It's Cloudy!

visit us at
www.abdopublishing.com

Published by ABDO Publishing Company, 8000 West 78th Street, Edina, Minnesota 55439.
Copyright © 2008 by Abdo Consulting Group, Inc. International copyrights reserved in all
countries. No part of this book may be reproduced in any form without written permission from the
publisher. The Checkerboard Library™ is a trademark and logo of ABDO Publishing Company.

Printed in the United States.

Cover Photo: iStockphoto
Interior Photos: Getty Images pp. 8, 28; iStockphoto pp. 1, 5, 7, 9, 17, 23, 27; NASA p. 29; National
    Oceanic and Atmospheric Administration/Department of Commerce pp. 13, 18, 19, 20, 21, 22,
    23, 24, 25, 26; Peter Arnold pp. 15, 27

Series Coordinator: Megan M. Gunderson
Editors: Rochelle Baltzer, Megan M. Gunderson
Art Direction & Cover Design: Neil Klinepier

Library of Congress Cataloging-in-Publication Data

Hirschmann, Kris, 1967-
  It's cloudy! / Kris Hirschmann.
    p. cm. -- (What's it like out?)
  Includes bibliographical references and index.
  ISBN 978-1-59928-943-4
  1. Clouds--Juvenile literature. I. Title.

QC921.35.H57 2008
551.57'6--dc22
                                        2007029156

Contents

It's Cloudy!

On a sunny day, three friends are lying in a field and pointing at the sky.

"It's a woolly lamb," says Daniel. "Do you see it?"

"It's not a lamb, it's a race car!" says Anna.

"No, it's a giant mushroom. I'm sure of it," says Sam.

Is there a lamb, a car, or a mushroom in the sky? Not really. These friends are talking about a puffy white cloud. The cloud has an **irregular** shape that reminds each of them of different things. Looking for these things is part of cloud watching, which is a favorite activity of people everywhere.

But not all clouds form airy sculptures. Some clouds are high and wispy. Others are low, gray, and sheetlike. Still others are huge columns that rise far into the sky. Clouds can create shady patches on a hot day. Or, they can spit out rain and snow. They can even sit right on the ground. So, the words "It's cloudy!" can mean many different things.

What do you see when you look up at the clouds?

What Are Clouds?

Many clouds look solid. But if you touched a cloud, your hand would go right through it! That's because clouds are just loose groups of water droplets or ice crystals.

The type of particles in a cloud depends on temperature. Above water's freezing point, or 32 degrees Fahrenheit (0°C), clouds contain water droplets. Below -40 degrees Fahrenheit (-40°C), clouds contain ice crystals.

Between the freezing point and -40 degrees, clouds may contain both ice crystals and water droplets. Water that remains liquid below the freezing point is called supercooled.

Cloud droplets are very tiny. Usually, there are a few hundred droplets in just .06 cubic inches (1 cu cm). But individually, all of a cloud's particles are very light. The gentlest breeze can push them upward. These upward-moving currents can also keep the droplets from falling to the ground.

Clouds may look like a thick, white mass.
Yet, even airplanes can fly right through them!

Water Vapor

Clouds could not exist without a gas called water vapor. This substance mixes with air when water from the earth's surface **evaporates**. We can't see water vapor, but it is around us all the time. Even the air we breathe contains water vapor.

The amount of water vapor in the air depends mostly on the air's temperature. At high temperatures, the air may contain a lot of vapor. These water molecules zip around quickly and stay in gas form.

At lower temperatures, water molecules slow down. They are more likely to **condense** or stick. When they condense, the vapor changes back into water droplets. This process removes water vapor from the air. For these reasons, cold air has a smaller **capacity** for water vapor than warm air.

Condensation happens at ground level, too. Water vapor in a warm bathroom condenses when it encounters a mirror's cool surface.

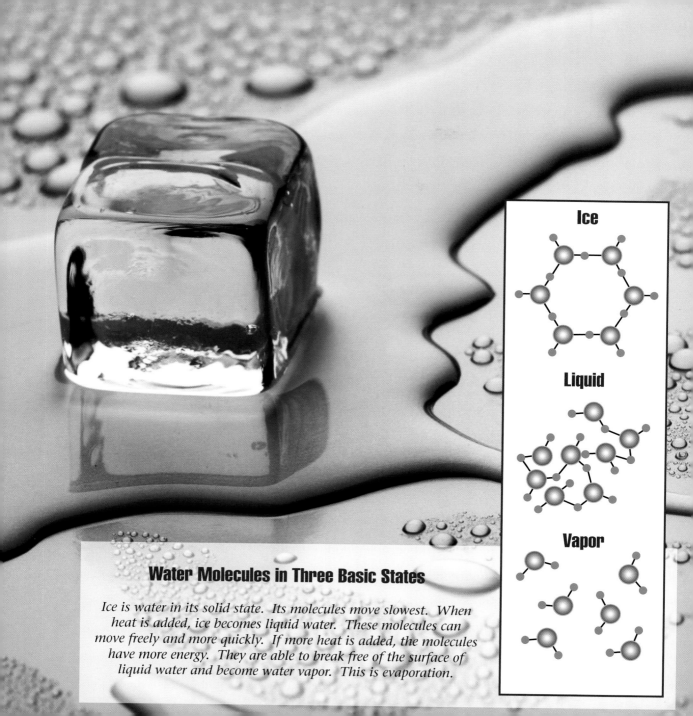

Ice

Liquid

Vapor

Water Molecules in Three Basic States

Ice is water in its solid state. Its molecules move slowest. When heat is added, ice becomes liquid water. These molecules can move freely and more quickly. If more heat is added, the molecules have more energy. They are able to break free of the surface of liquid water and become water vapor. This is evaporation.

Rising Air

Water vapor enters the air near ground level. It **evaporates** from bodies of water all over Earth. If conditions are right, water vapor may rise high into the sky and form clouds. There are four main ways this can happen.

Convection is one reason clouds form. In this process, the sun heats the earth's surface, which then warms the air directly above it. In warm air, water molecules move faster than in cold air. And, warm air is less **dense** and lighter than cooler air. So the warm air floats upward, carrying water vapor with it.

Convection

Orographic Lifting

Geography can make air rise through a process called orographic (awr-uh-GRA-fihk) lifting. Air is forced upward as it travels over mountains, hills, or ridges. A load of water vapor travels upward with the air.

The meeting of warm and cold **fronts** is another reason for rising air. Sometimes, cold fronts meet warmer air. When they do, the heavier cold air wedges under the lighter warm air. When a warm front encounters colder air, it lifts over the air. Both of these movements cause water vapor to rise through frontal lifting.

Convergence is the fourth reason for rising air. During convergence, air rushes inward toward the same spot. This causes air at the center point to move skyward.

Frontal Lifting   **Convergence**

A Cloud Is Born

A cloud begins with low-level air. The air may be full of water vapor, but it does not yet look cloudy. In fact, it may look perfectly clear near ground level.

As the air rises, it expands and cools. As the air cools to below the **dew point**, it becomes **supersaturated**. Then, the water vapor may begin **condensing** into liquid droplets. If the temperature is low enough, the water vapor may even freeze into ice crystals. As droplets or crystals form, a brand new cloud appears.

This process would not be possible without airborne bits of salt, dust, and other matter. These

HUMIDITY

Relative humidity describes the amount of water vapor in the air compared to how much it can hold. When air contains all the water vapor it possibly can, the relative humidity is 100 percent. This means the air is saturated.

The amount of water vapor the air can hold changes with temperature. So, relative humidity may change even if the amount of water vapor in the air does not. For example, if the temperature falls, the air has a lower capacity for water. So the air is closer to being saturated, even though the amount of water vapor has not changed.

Calculating the dew point is another way to measure humidity. The dew point is the temperature at which the air containing a certain amount of water vapor will become saturated. Little difference between air temperature and the dew point means an uncomfortable, humid day!

particles are called cloud **condensation** nuclei. Water vapor condenses onto them. If you could magnify cloud droplets and crystals many hundreds of times, you would see a solid nucleus at the center of every one.

Clouds form as the air temperature drops below the dew point.

6,000 feet
Temperature: 60°F
Dew Point: 60°F

3,000 feet
Temperature: 76°F
Dew Point: 60°F

Surface
Temperature: 92°F
Dew Point: 60°F

A Cloud's Life

Once clouds form, they may do many different things. If the surrounding air is dry, they may disappear quickly. If the air is damp, they may hang around for a long time. A newborn cloud may keep its shape if winds are light. But if winds are strong, it may change shape or spread apart.

Warm, rising air pumps some clouds full of energy. As they grow, water droplets and ice crystals collide and begin sticking together. Soon, the particles are too heavy to be supported by the air rising in the cloud. They fall and may reach the ground as rain, snow, hail, or other types of precipitation.

At the end of its life cycle, a cloud enters the **dissipating** stage. Air leaves the cloud through **downdrafts** but does not return through **updrafts**. Conditions calm down inside the cloud, and growth slows to a stop. The precipitation may continue for a while, and then the cloud breaks up.

During a cloud's mature stage, updrafts feed the cloud while rain and strong downdrafts form.

Naming Clouds

All clouds form in the same basic way. But they do not all look the same. Clouds can take various shapes. And, they can be found at many different altitudes. Scientists use a simple system to describe these differences.

The first part of the system uses Latin words to describe a cloud's shape. Puffy clouds are called cumulus, from a word meaning "heap" or "pile." Flat or layered clouds are called stratus, meaning "to

THE CLOUD CLASSIFICATION SYSTEM

English meteorologist Luke Howard designed the modern cloud classification system. Published in 1803, his work describes the shapes of cirrus, cumulus, and stratus clouds. Today, scientists also use other Latin words to describe a cloud's behavior.

castellanus = castle-like, with tall turrets connected by a common base

congestus = pile up, heap up, accumulate

humilis = humble, low to the ground, small

lenticularis = lens-shaped

mediocris = medium-sized

nimbus = rainy cloud

uncinus = hooked like a comma, with the top ending in a tuft or a hook

undulatus = forming in waves

Fog is a cloud at ground level.

spread out." And feathery clouds are called cirrus, which means "curl" or "tuft."

These words can be used on their own or combined with others. For example, a high, veil-like cloud layer is called cirrostratus. Layered, puffy clouds are named stratocumulus.

The second part of the system describes a cloud's altitude. Most clouds are said to be low, middle, or high. Clouds that grow upward through the levels are called vertical clouds.

Low Clouds

Low clouds are found less than 6,500 feet (2,000 m) above the earth's surface. The classic low cloud is a flat, gray layer called stratus. Stratus clouds can be made of water droplets or ice crystals, depending on the temperature. They may cause some drizzle or mist.

Sometimes, stratus clouds begin to produce rain. This means a nimbostratus has developed. Nimbostratus clouds are flat on the bottom and dark. They bring steady rain or snow,

Stratus

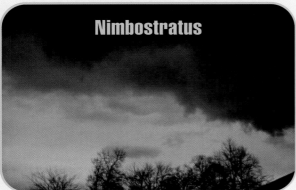

Nimbostratus

which can last for a day or even longer. Nimbostratus are considered middle clouds, but they may be found closer to the ground.

Stratocumulus clouds are gray, puffy, and low. They may be separated by areas of blue sky and sunlight. But they can fill the sky, crowding together into a sun-blocking layer. Stratocumulus clouds may look threatening, but they are not storm clouds.

Stratocumulus

Rather, they often appear after a storm passes. So, these clouds are usually a sign that the weather is improving.

Middle Clouds

Middle clouds are found between 6,500 and 23,000 feet (2,000 and 7,000 m) above the earth's surface. They can be made of water droplets, ice crystals, or both.

Altostratus clouds are one member of the middle cloud group. Like stratus clouds, altostratus clouds form dreary layers that cover the sky. But, these layers are much higher up. The sun can shine faintly through an altostratus sheet. But, you will not see your shadow under these clouds. And, they may be a sign that steady rain is headed your way.

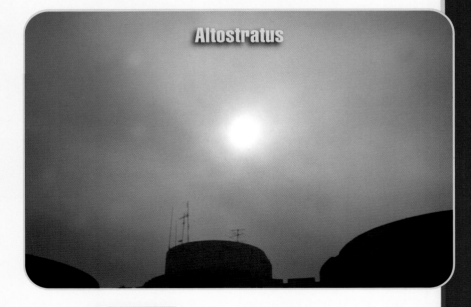

Altostratus

Altocumulus

Altocumulus clouds are another type of middle cloud. They are small, puffy, and appear white or gray. They often group together to form bands or wave patterns. Altocumulus clouds may line up with the wind, forming cloud streets. These clouds can be beautiful, especially at sunrise and sunset. But watch out! They usually mean rain is coming.

High Clouds

High clouds are found between 16,500 and 45,000 feet (5,000 and 13,000 m) above the earth's surface. The air temperature at these heights is very cool. So, high clouds are usually made of ice crystals.

Cirrus clouds are a common type of high cloud. They are white and wispy. Wind can pull them into long strands called mare's tails. Cirrus clouds usually signal a change in the weather.

Cirrus

Cirrocumulus

Cirrocumulus clouds may indicate storms are on the way. They are small and rounded. And when they crowd together in a repetitive pattern, they

Cirrostratus

resemble fish scales. For this reason, a sky filled with cirrocumulus clouds is called a mackerel sky.

Another type of high cloud may also mean rain is coming. Cirrostratus clouds are thin, icy layers that make the whole sky look hazy. The sun and the moon can shine through this veil. When this happens, they seem to be surrounded by colorful rings called halos. **Sun dogs** may also occur when cirrostratus clouds are present.

Sun Dogs and a Halo

Vertical Clouds

Some clouds do not fit neatly into an altitude category. Vertical clouds can stretch through many levels of the sky. They form by convection. Vertical clouds are common on warm days, when there is plenty of hot air to feed their growth.

Cumulus

The fluffy, floating cotton balls you see forming on warm mornings are called cumulus clouds. Cumulus clouds have low, flat bases. But, their tops bubble upward during the growth phase. They start to look more like cauliflowers than cotton balls. They grow and **merge** to become cumulus congestus clouds. These easily reach the sky's middle level.

Sometimes, cumulus clouds stop growing. But if conditions are right, they don't. As the day gets hotter, cumulus clouds can get bigger and taller. They may rise 60,000 feet (18,000 m) above the ground! These huge vertical formations are called cumulonimbus clouds.

Cumulonimbus clouds are lovely and dramatic. But, they are also dangerous. They can bring severe storms that produce rain, lightning, thunder, hail, and even tornadoes.

Cumulonimbus

Unusual Clouds

Clouds can form odd shapes. Cumulonimbus clouds may be flat on top, like **anvils**. When air inside the clouds pushes downward, they may develop round bumps on their undersides. These are called mammatus clouds. Rotating mammatus may be a sign of severe weather. But, these clouds may also signal that severe weather is ending.

Anvil

Mammatus

Altocumulus clouds can look unusual, as well. For instance, saucer-shaped altocumulus may form near mountains. These clouds are round and flattened, with perfectly smooth edges. They can look like UFOs! These strange formations are called lenticular clouds.

Another unusual cloud formation is the **condensation** trail, or contrail. Contrails are long, straight cloud streaks. They form when water vapor in a jet airplane's **exhaust** condenses.

Contrail streaks are thin and sharp at first. But if there are high-level winds, contrails are soon pulled apart. They spread into loose bands that stretch across the sky. Or if the air is too dry, they **evaporate**.

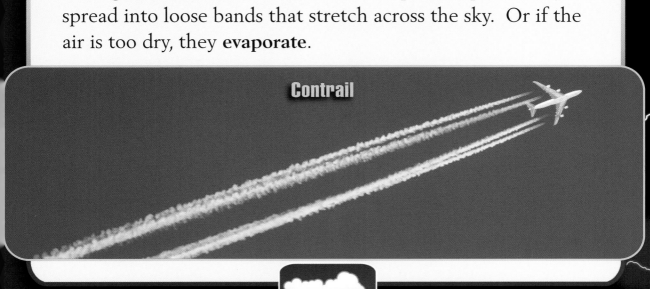
Contrail

Important Jobs

With so many shapes and sizes, clouds are fun to watch. But clouds also have many important jobs to do. Cooling the earth is one of these jobs. High, thin clouds let in and trap sunlight. This warms the earth. Low, thick clouds reflect a lot of incoming sunlight back into space. Without this balance, average temperatures on Earth would be much higher.

Clouds are also vital to Earth's hydrologic cycle. This is the process that moves water from Earth's surface to the

atmosphere and back again. Clouds help carry moisture from Earth's surface to the sky. When they drift, the moisture moves with them. They return the moisture to Earth as precipitation, such as rain or snow.

Storm spotters watch for wall clouds or rotation in clouds that might indicate severe weather, such as a tornado.

Clouds can even help people **predict** the weather. Changes in cloud conditions are especially useful indicators of an oncoming storm.

First, you may see cirrus clouds thicken and **merge** to form cirrostratus clouds. Then, these clouds are hidden or replaced by thickening altostratus clouds. This brings light precipitation. Nimbostratus may form next, bringing even heavier precipitation.

So the next time it's cloudy outside, pay attention to the sky. What type of weather is on the way? It's written in the clouds!

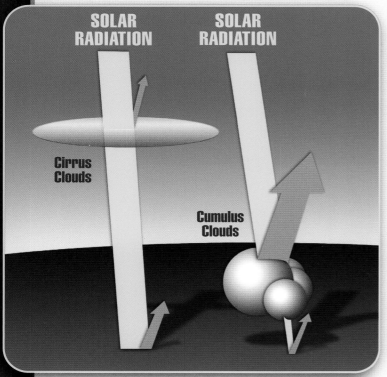

SOLAR RADIATION

SOLAR RADIATION

Cirrus Clouds

Cumulus Clouds

High, thin clouds such as cirrus clouds let in solar radiation. Low, thick clouds such as cumulus clouds reflect it back into space.

Glossary

anvil - a heavy iron block used for shaping metal. Or, anything resembling an anvil in shape, such as a cumulonimbus cloud with a flat top.

capacity - the maximum amount of something that can be held or contained.

condense - to change from a gas or a vapor into a liquid or a solid, usually caused by a decrease in temperature.

dense - having a high mass per unit volume.

dew point - the temperature at which water vapor begins condensing.

dissipate - to break up or scatter and disappear.

downdraft - a downward movement of gas, such as air.

evaporate - to change from a liquid or a solid into a vapor.

exhaust - used gas or vapor that escapes from an engine.

front - an advancing edge of an air mass.

irregular - lacking evenness or a specific pattern.

merge - to combine or blend.

predict - to guess something ahead of time on the basis of observation, experience, or reasoning.

sun dog - also called a parhelion. A bright, often colorful spot caused by light shining through ice crystals in the atmosphere. It is seen on either side of the sun.

supersaturated - filled beyond saturation, such as when air has been cooled to below the temperature at which it contains the maximum amount of water.

updraft - an upward movement of gas, such as air.

Web Sites

To learn more about weather, visit ABDO Publishing Company on the World Wide Web at **www.abdopublishing.com**. Web sites about weather are featured on our Book Links page. These links are routinely monitored and updated to provide the most current information available.

Index